GO WILD
IN THE
MOUNTAINS

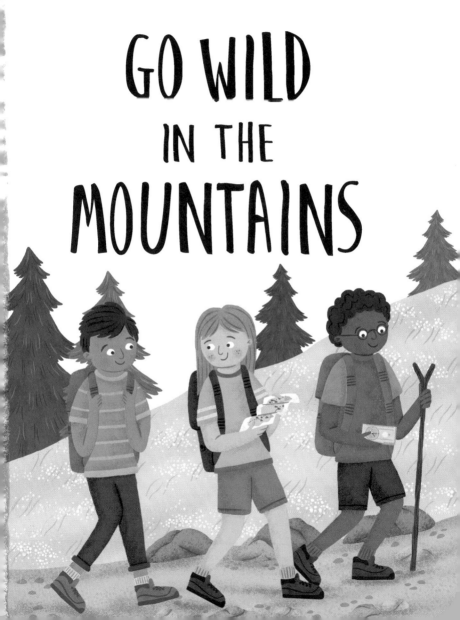

First published 2020 by Nosy Crow Ltd
The Crow's Nest, 14 Baden Place
Crosby Row, London, SE1 1YW
www.nosycrow.com

ISBN 978 1 78800 642 2

Nosy Crow and associated logos are trademarks
and/or registered trademarks of Nosy Crow Ltd.

Text © Goldie Hawk 2020
Illustrations © Rachael Saunders 2020

A CIP catalogue record for this book is available from the British Library.

Printed in China
Papers used by Nosy Crow are made from wood grown
in sustainable forests.

1 3 5 7 9 8 6 4 2

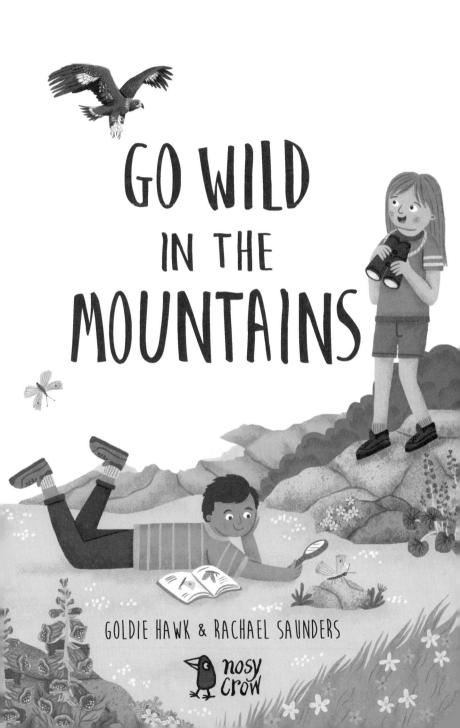

GO WILD
IN THE
MOUNTAINS

GOLDIE HAWK & RACHAEL SAUNDERS

nosy crow

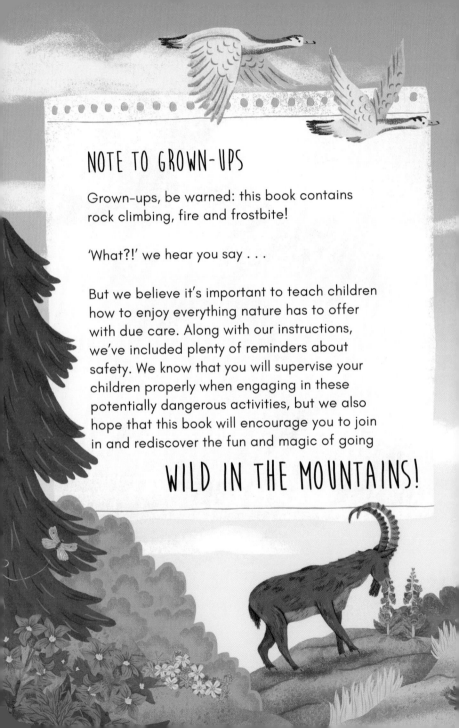

NOTE TO GROWN-UPS

Grown-ups, be warned: this book contains rock climbing, fire and frostbite!

'What?!' we hear you say . . .

But we believe it's important to teach children how to enjoy everything nature has to offer with due care. Along with our instructions, we've included plenty of reminders about safety. We know that you will supervise your children properly when engaging in these potentially dangerous activities, but we also hope that this book will encourage you to join in and rediscover the fun and magic of going

WILD IN THE MOUNTAINS!

Mountains are wild, magical places, with amazing creatures, from golden eagles to grey wolves. Here you will discover beautiful views, perilous peaks and amazing wildlife that has adapted to some of the harshest conditions in the world. Perhaps you'll go hiking or mountain biking in the summer. Maybe you'll build an igloo or go skiing in the winter. Whatever you do, I hope this book helps you love our mountains and everything on them even more.

So go on — it's time to get out into nature and enjoy the marvellous mountains!

GOLDIE HAWK

CONTENTS

ARE YOU READY TO GO WILD IN THE MOUNTAINS?

Do you love adventure, getting outdoors and reaching new heights? Then this is the book for you!

In this ultimate guide, you will find lots of fun activities to do in the mountains, from hiking, skiing and mountain biking to finding mountain animals and wildlife. You will also learn exactly what not to do, from getting attacked by mountain lions to getting caught in an avalanche.

This book is about being safe and having fun. But it's also about having adventures. You should be willing to get a bit muddy and smelly and you absolutely must be good at working in a team.

There are three important rules for going wild in the mountains:

1. When in doubt, DON'T!
2. Always ask your grown-up
3. Have fun!

Are you ready for your alpine adventure to begin?
Then . . . LET'S GO WILD!

WHAT IS A MOUNTAIN?

A mountain is an area of land that rises high above the ground, with steep, sloping sides and a 'summit', or peak, at the top. Most scientists agree that a mountain must be at least 305 metres high. That's about the height of 62 double-decker buses stacked on top of each other!

Most mountains are millions of years old and they can be found on all continents of the world, usually in groups called 'ranges'.

There are lots of different ways that mountains can be created, but all of them start deep underground where there is a layer of hot, molten rock called 'magma'. Magma makes the tectonic plates of the Earth's crust move.

FOLD MOUNTAIN

Very occasionally these tectonic plates push against each other, causing their edges to crumple and squeeze the ground up. This creates a tall, jagged 'fold mountain'.

BLOCK MOUNTAIN

Sometimes the moving plates push a block of rock up between them. This makes a wedge-shaped 'block mountain'.

DOME MOUNTAIN

Sometimes magma (molten rock) pushes its way up under the Earth's crust. If it's unable to crack through the surface it creates a bulging 'dome mountain'.

magma

VOLCANIC MOUNTAIN

Sometimes magma erupts through a crack in the Earth's crust, creating a volcano! The magma turns to lava, which piles up, cools and hardens into rock to make a 'volcanic mountain'.

WHAT YOU WILL NEED IN THE MOUNTAINS

The ultimate mountain explorer needs the right gear. Not too much or you won't be able to carry it up the mountain; not too little or you won't be prepared.

WHAT TO TAKE:

- Maps
- Compass
- Mobile phone (for emergencies)
- Penknife
- Rope or cord
- First aid kit: bandages, scissors, antiseptic wipes, tape, blister plasters, safety pins, medical tape
- Sun cream
- Lip balm
- Food

- Snacks (cereal bars, nuts, dried fruit)
- Torch or headtorch
- Waterproof matches
- Portable cooking stove
- Water purification tablets
- Whistle
- Tent and sleeping bag (if you're camping)
- Water bottle filled with drinking water
- Camera
- Binoculars

WHAT NOT TO TAKE:
Your pet goldfish; a microwave; a saxophone; a scooter; your school photo.

WHAT TO WEAR

Usually, you'll need a mix of summer and winter clothing. Even if it's warm at the bottom of the mountain, it might be snowing at the top.

SUMMER:

- T-shirt or long-sleeved top
- Comfortable shorts or trousers
- Jumper
- Coat
- Waterproof coat in case it rains
- Walking boots
- Walking socks
- Swimming costume or trunks
- Sunglasses
- Sun hat

WINTER:

- Thermal top and trousers
- Ski trousers
- Jumpers
- Ski jacket
- Snow boots or walking boots
- Warm socks
- Scarf
- Gloves
- Sunglasses or ski goggles
- Warm hat

WHAT NOT TO WEAR:
A ball gown; nothing but your underwear; a shiny spacesuit; pyjamas.

HIKING IN THE MOUNTAINS

The first thing to do when planning a hike is to find a group of friends. You never know what might happen in the mountains, so you need a trustworthy team that will work together.

Next, you need to decide which mountain to hike up. If it's your first hike, you should choose a mountain that isn't too high or steep — you'll need a bit of practice before you set off for Everest!

Calculate how long it will take you to reach the top and come back down (don't forget to include time for breaks) and decide whether you're going to camp overnight.

REMEMBER
Don't forget to tell someone where you're going and how long you think you'll be.

Next, check the weather. You don't want to get caught in a storm or blizzard! The best time to go on your hike is when the sky is clear and it's not too cold.

How to pack a hiking rucksack

There is an art to packing your hiking rucksack. You want to have the heaviest things at the bottom and the lightest things at the top. And your first aid kit and torch need to be easy to find, in case of emergencies.

Top: clothes and sleeping bag

Side pockets: torch, first aid kit, penknife

Middle: food and cooking equipment

Bottom: tent (if you're taking one), other heavy things (just leave out the rocks!)

Attached to bag: tarp, bucket and lightweight cooking grill

NAVIGATION

To find your way in the mountains, you need to know how to read a map. It's not as tricky as you might think. Here's what you need to know.

KEY

Most maps have a key. This is like a code to tell you where things are. On mountain maps, a key will tell you where to find walking trails, cycle trails, viewpoints and any mountain huts or stop-off points along the way.

building

river

camping

road

deciduous tree

path

conifer

bridge

wooden fence

SCALE

It's impossible for a map to show the land in its actual size, so everything is drawn a lot smaller. This is called 'drawing to scale'. Maps come in different scales that are written on the front. If a map has a scale of 1:10,000, this means that one centimetre on the map represents 10,000 centimetres (or 100 metres) in real life.

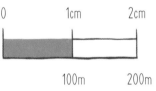

0   1cm   2cm

100m   200m

HOW NOT TO READ A MAP: upside down; on the toilet; in the dark.

CONTOUR LINES

Contour lines are drawn onto maps to show how steep or shallow the land is, and how challenging it will be to walk up. If contour lines are drawn close together, it means the land is steep. If contour lines are drawn far apart, the land is flat.

HOW TO USE A COMPASS

You can usually find your way using Global Positioning Systems (GPS). This is what we use when we navigate using maps on our mobile phones. But what happens if your battery runs down or you have no signal? In case that happens, it's essential to know how to use a map and compass. Plus, it's much more fun!

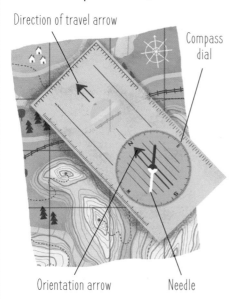

Direction of travel arrow

Compass dial

Orientation arrow

Needle

There are four main points on your compass. In clockwise order these are: north, east, south, and west. (You can remember this by saying "Never Eat Slimy Worms".) The measurements marked on the outside of the compass are called 'degrees' and they are used to find your 'bearing', the angle of direction between where you are heading and North.

The most important part of the compass is the magnetic needle. It swings around the compass dial as you move, but when it settles the red end always points north. The arrow attached to 'North' on the compass dial is known as the 'orientation arrow' and the arrow on the baseplate is called the 'direction of travel arrow'.

To walk in an exact direction, you can 'follow a bearing':

1. Place your compass flat on the map, with the direction of travel arrow pointing to where you want to go.

2. Twist your compass dial so that the orienting arrow faces where North is on your map.

3. The direction of travel arrow should line up with the number of degrees on the compass dial to give you your 'bearing'. Take the compass off the map and turn around with the compass until the red magnetic needle lines up with the orientation arrow.

4. Now you can begin your walk! Follow the direction of travel arrow, trying to keep the orienting arrow lined up with the magnetic needle as you move. (Remember to keep your compass dial in the same position to help you stay on track!)

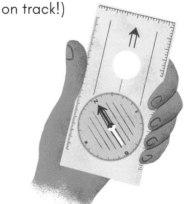

FINDING AND MAKING A HIKING STICK

You can make your very own hiking stick out of discarded wood. If you're using a knife to cut it down, remember knives are VERY dangerous. ALWAYS point the knife blade away from you and, if you're uncertain how to cut something correctly, ask your grown-up to help you.

1. Find a suitable stick. It should be strong and roughly come up to your armpit.

2. If it's too long, use a knife to carefully trim it down to the right size.

3. If you want, you can (carefully) shave the bark off using a penknife to make the stick smoother and more comfortable to grip.

4. Now you're all set to go!

WHAT NOT TO DO WITH YOUR STICK: harm an animal; harm a person; poke your friend; pick your nose.

CLIMBING STEEP PATHS

Climbing might sound easy, but you may reach some steep areas during your hike. Make sure you pace yourself and stop for breaks if you or your team members get tired.

If you come across obstacles, such as fallen trees or big rocks, speak to your team and decide whether it's safe to climb or whether you should take a different route.

Don't forget: what goes up, must come down. Climbing down mountains can be even more difficult than climbing up!

DID YOU KNOW?
When people mountaineer in the Himalayas, they often employ local Sherpa people – who are excellent climbers – as guides.

CROSSING A STREAM

On your hike, you may need to cross a stream. If it's just a trickle of water, you don't need to worry. But if it's more than ankle-deep, you must be careful.

Check how deep the water is by using your hiking stick. If you're worried, have a look to see if there is a shallower place to cross. And if the water is rushing past quickly, look for a different route.

If the stream is calm and no more than knee deep, carefully step into the water, using your stick to check for anything hidden under the surface that might make you trip. Next, make slow, sideways steps diagonally upstream until you reach the other side.

LEARN SOME MOUNTAINEERING KNOTS

When you're hiking in the mountains, it's useful to know some mountaineering knots! Professional mountain climbers often rope themselves to their team in case anyone falls. But ropes can also be used for tying your bag to a tree when you camp, or to help any of your team who are struggling to climb steep slopes.

FIGURE OF EIGHT LOOP

This knot creates a strong loop, which is very handy if you want to hang something from a tree or attach a rope to a carabiner. A carabiner is a special clip used for abseiling or climbing.

1. Double your rope back on itself. This will create a loop.

3. Bring the looped end around the tail of the rope and up through the eye.

2. Bring the looped end under the tail of the rope to create another loop. This is called the 'eye'.

4. Pull the knot tight!

DOUBLE FISHERMAN'S KNOT

This knot is used to tie two ropes together or join two ends of one rope to create a strong loop. To make things easier, use two differently coloured ropes.

1. Lie the ends of the ropes together.

2. Loop the yellow rope over the red rope twice and push the end through the loops.

3. Loop the red rope over the yellow rope twice and push the end through the loops.

4. Tighten the two separate knots by pulling on their ends.

5. Pull the main lengths of the yellow and red ropes to bring the knots close together.

SETTING UP CAMP IN THE MOUNTAINS

If you're hiking in the summer, you might want to camp overnight!

HOW TO PITCH YOUR TENT

Before you pitch your tent, you should assess your camping ground. You don't want to topple down the mountain in the middle of the night and you won't be very comfortable if you're sleeping on bumpy or soggy patches. So look for a level piece of ground, a good distance away from any puddles or steep drops.

SURVIVAL TIP
Flat and dry,
happy guy.
Wet and hilly,
feeling silly.

It's also a good idea to make sure that your tent doorway is facing away from any incoming wind or rain. A beautiful mountain view is nice too!

Not all tents are the same. Some pop up, some can be inflated and some need ropes and poles. But all should come with instructions — just remember to bring them with you, or you'll be in a bit of a pickle! Why not practise setting up your tent in your back garden before you go? That way, you won't need to spend hours pitching your tent up the mountain or have arguments about which pole goes where.

WHERE NOT TO PITCH YOUR TENT:
on the side of a mountain; on a hill; on a rock (unless you want a very uncomfortable night's sleep).

STARTING A FIRE

You'll need a fire to prepare drinking water, cook food and keep warm. But you must remember these golden safety rules:

1. Always keep some water nearby so you can put out your fire if you need to.

2. Tie back long hair (unless you want a dodgy haircut!).

3. Make sure you always put out your fire completely when you leave the area.

4. If a spark lands on your clothes or you find yourself on fire, don't run around flapping your arms! Oxygen will fuel the flames and make them bigger. Instead, STOP, DROP AND ROLL! Smother the flames with a blanket.

5. Never start a fire without a grown-up.

First of all, clear an area of grass, leaves and twigs. Next, create a ring of stones where your fire will be. This will stop it spreading!

YOU WILL NEED:

1. Tinder: small, dry stuff, such as dry grass, pine needles, feathers, cotton balls.

2. Kindling: bigger bits of dry stuff, such as pieces of split wood, pine cones, dry leaves, cotton rags.

3. Firewood: logs, fallen branches.

Make a small pile of tinder, then place the kindling in a teepee shape over it. Add logs to make a bigger teepee shape, then light the tinder with a match. Gently blow on the flames to get them blazing!

FINDING WATER IN THE MOUNTAINS

You get much more dehydrated up in the mountains, so it's important to drink plenty of water. Luckily, water is easy to find. All mountains have rivers. In fact, a lot of the water we drink comes from them!

All you need to do is find a river or stream. Avoid stagnant water — water is only safe to drink when it's moving.

Even though mountain water is as fresh as can be, it isn't necessarily safe to drink straight from streams because there's a chance it might have bacteria in it. Drinking it might make you sick. To be safe, you should boil it for several minutes and wait for it to cool down, or add a water purification tablet.

HOW TO COOK IN THE MOUNTAINS

You'll use up a lot of energy hiking in the mountains, so you need to eat a lot.

Professional mountaineers pack freeze-dried meals. Freeze drying removes all the water from the food, so it's light to carry. You can get all kinds of dehydrated meals, from spaghetti bolognese to chocolate pudding. You just need to add water and cook over your portable stove.

As well as meals, snacks like dried fruit and cereal bars will give you lots of energy along the way. Try this hearty meal traditionally eaten in the Alps.

SURVIVAL TIP
Always wash your hands before you cook and eat — especially if you've just been to the loo!

COOK A CHEESE FONDUE

YOU WILL NEED:
• 400 g hard mountain cheese (such as gruyère or emmental)
• Half a lemon
• 1 clove of garlic, peeled and chopped in half
• Bread, chopped into bite-sized cubes
• Cooking pot
• Cheese grater
• Skewers or long forks

1. Rub the inside of the cooking pot with the cut sides of the garlic clove, then throw away the garlic.

2. Squeeze the juice of half a lemon into the pot.

3. Carefully grate all the cheese into the pot.

4. Melt the cheese over the stove, stirring in a zigzag pattern.

5. Once your cheese is melted, turn off your stove.

6. Now stick the bread cubes onto the skewers or forks and dip into the fondue.

7. Eat!

You can dip other foods into the fondue too, such as cherry tomatoes, roasted baby potatoes or apple chunks.

SUMMER MOUNTAIN ACTIVITIES

MOUNTAIN BIKING

You don't need to own a bike to go mountain biking. Most mountain resorts will have a bike shop where you can rent your bike and helmet. Mountain bikes are different from normal bikes because they have tougher wheels and more suspension, which means it's less jolty when riding over bumps.

The most important thing to remember when you're riding in the mountains is to look ahead, not down, because you may have to dodge obstacles. Keep your eyes out for rocks, steep turns or low branches.

When you're cycling uphill, lean forward and try to stay seated to keep yourself balanced. When you're cycling downhill, you can stand up off the seat, making sure your pedals are parallel to the ground.

TOP TIP
Choose lower gears when you're cycling uphill and higher gears when you're cycling downhill.

You must also make sure you brake properly. When you're going downhill, don't brake too hard or you might skid or tip over the handlebars. Instead, shift your weight back and brake gently.

29

ROCK CLIMBING

Rock climbing is a really fun activity, but it's also dangerous. You should always climb with a guide, wearing a harness and a helmet.

You can practise rock climbing at a climbing centre. These have soft mats underneath the climbing walls, so it doesn't matter if you fall.

1. Place your foot in your first foothold and use your fingers to grip the handhold. Then look for another foothold and handhold and begin your climb. Make sure you push yourself up with your legs rather than your arms.

2. Keep your arms extended while looking for new footholds, otherwise you might strain your upper arms.

3. Keep your hips close to the wall and point your knees to the side so that you're not putting your weight on your fingers and arms. Your hands should only be used for balance, not to pull yourself up.

4. If you think you cannot go any further, let your guide know and come back down. But don't forget to admire the view first!

DID YOU KNOW?
Some professional climbers scale frozen waterfalls with nothing but ice picks and shoe studs to help!

WHAT NOT TO DO
WHEN YOU ABSEIL:
dance; attempt aerial
acrobatics; have a snooze.

DID YOU KNOW?
Some very experienced
mountaineers abseil
without a harness!

ABSEILING

Abseiling — also known as 'rappelling' — is when a person descends a rock face or climbing wall using a rope and harness. It should only be done with an instructor and you'll need a helmet in case you bash your head!

Your instructor will show you how to abseil, but here are the basic steps:

1. Once your harness has been checked by your instructor, you will be attached to two ropes, a rope for you to abseil down and a safety line.

2. There will be someone standing below the rock face, holding on to the safety line and making sure you don't get hurt.

3. When you are told to do so, lean backward over the drop, keeping your knees together, and start to lower yourself, using your feet to step down the rock face.

4. Keep an eye out for obstacles and keep looking behind you to check how far away you are from the ground.

FISHING

Mountain lakes are the perfect place for freshwater fishing, so why not give it a go? Remember, lots of fishing spots are privately owned, so make sure you have permission first.

1. Cast your line by bringing the rod to your side and swinging it smoothly in the direction you want to fish (and without whacking anyone in the process!).

REMEMBER
To go fishing, anyone over the age of 12 needs a rod licence. Find out more at:
www.gov.uk/ fishing-licences

2. Wait. This bit takes patience and you have to be quiet because fish are startled by loud noises.

3. If you feel or see the rod jerk, you might have caught a fish. Reel in the line and see what you've hooked.

WHAT YOU MIGHT CATCH:
brown trout;
grayling; char;
rainbow trout.

WHAT YOU WON'T CATCH:
a shark; a trombone;
a hockey stick; a
diamond ring (unless
you're very lucky).

4. If you don't feel a bite after 10–15 minutes, reel in your line and cast it again.

SWIMMING IN LAKES

If it's nice and hot in the mountains, why not go for a dip? There's nothing better than cooling off in fresh alpine water after a long hike.

But while swimming in mountain lakes can be great fun, you absolutely must be careful, even if you're a strong swimmer. Always go with a grown-up and make sure you follow this checklist:

• Make sure you only swim in safe, designated swimming areas, ideally where there are life guards.
• Never swim without your grown-up.
• Test the water first to check it's not too cold (some mountain lakes are freezing!).

If you find you have swum too far from the shore, stay calm. If you panic and flap your arms, you'll waste energy and may even push yourself underwater. Instead, take even breaths, remain afloat and try to swim back towards the shore while calling for help. Your friends and grown-up can use a rope to pull you out.

WHAT TO WEAR:
swimwear or wetsuit; goggles; old soft or surf shoes to protect your feet.

WHAT NOT TO WEAR:
a ski jacket; crash helmet; roller skates; dinosaur onesie.

CANOEING

A great way to explore a mountain river or lake is to travel in a canoe! You should be able to rent your canoe from a nearby water sports shop, and you'll need a life jacket too.

1. Carefully get into your canoe.

2. Hold your paddle with a light grip, so that your knuckles are in line with the blade.

3. Dip your paddle into the water on your right side and push the water behind you. Then do the same on the left side. Repeat this right-left right-left rhythm to power forward in a straight line.

WATERFALL WARNING!
Some mountain rivers lead to waterfalls. These can be great fun to explore . . . if you know they're there!

4. If you want to steer left, paddle more on your right side; if you want to steer right, paddle more on your left.

DO:
stay close to land; listen to your grown-up; make sure your life jacket and helmet are fitted properly.

DON'T:
try to capsize; do a spot of yoga; splash your friends; go anywhere near a waterfall.

WHITE-WATER RAFTING

If you like an adrenalin rush, you'll love white-water rafting! It takes place on white water rapids, which are fast-flowing areas of a river where the water is white and frothy.

White water rafts are large inflatable boats made of rubber that usually seat about five people.

You will need to sit in your raft as instructed by your guide and paddle using an oar, keeping hold of the T-grip at the top. Your guide will tell you which direction to go in, but you will need to dodge any rocks, and if anyone shouts "Hold on", hold on tightly to the side of the raft.

If you fall in (you probably will), close your mouth and keep calm! Your life jacket will keep you afloat but try to position yourself so you're on your back, facing up and with your toes out of the water. Your friends or guide should be able to pull you back on to the raft.

REMEMBER
Always go with a guide, wear a life jacket, helmet and water shoes . . . and prepare to get soaked!

WINTER MOUNTAIN ACTIVITIES

SKIING FOR BEGINNERS

Skiing is super fun but takes a bit of time to master. Before you go to the mountains, you can have lessons at a dry ski slope.

It will feel strange standing up on skis at first. Get used to it by sliding them forward and backward on flat ground. You might fall over a few times, but as long as the snow isn't too icy, this won't hurt!

TOP TIP
When you become more confident, you can start using ski poles. These keep you balanced and can be used to push you along.

1. Bend your knees slightly, place your hands on your thighs and look straight ahead. If there are lots of other skiers setting off, wait for them to go so you have a quiet slope.

2. Start sliding down the slope, aiming diagonally downhill   you want to make 'S' shapes as you ski, moving from one side of the slope to the other.

3. Angle your skis so that the tips are close together but your feet are shoulder-width apart. Your skis should form the shape of a pizza slice. This is called a 'snow plough'.

4. Your weight should be slightly forward. If you feel the weight on your heels, lean forward by pushing your shins against the front of your boots.

5. When you get to the edge of the piste, slowly turn, keeping your skis in a pizza slice shape. Gently push more with your right leg to turn left and more with your left leg to turn right.

6. Make sure you don't turn with your shoulders as you might lose balance!

7. If you want to stop, make your pizza slice shape bigger by pushing the backs of the skis wider.

SKIING FOR PROS

Once you've mastered the snow plough, you can try skiing in 'parallel'. This is when your skis are an equal distance apart, like railway lines.

1. Try to keep your skis no more than hip-width apart, with your arms out to the side, not touching your body and your poles pointing backward.

2. Just like when you ski in snow plough, you should gently bend your knees and start skiing diagonally down the slope, aiming to make slightly smaller 'S' shapes as you go down.

3. Your weight will naturally fall more on one leg than the other. If you're skiing diagonally left, you will lean left, with the edge of your left ski digging slightly into the snow. If you're skiing to the right, you will do the same on your right ski.

4. To turn, lean forward, bringing your weight on to both skis. Then you need to shift your weight over to the other side. So, if you have been skiing to the left and you want to turn to the right, then you need to lean over to the right, while pushing on your outside (downhill) ski.

5. If you reach a very steep part of the slope, you can go back to snow plough, or slide down the slope sideways, keeping your skis parallel.

REMEMBER
If you don't wear sunglasses or goggles, you could end up with sun or snow blindness. This is when the sun's ultraviolet rays burn your eyes!

HOW NOT TO SKI:
backward; on someone's shoulders; with one leg in the air.

SNOWBOARDING

Snowboarding can be tricky, but with a bit of patience and practise, you'll soon be a boarding pro!

First, practise by slowly sliding down the slope with your board horizontal. Once you feel more confident, you can start going down the mountain with one foot forward.

1. Position your board so you have one foot in front of the other and the board is facing diagonally down the slope, with your body sideways to the slope.

2. Bend your knees and keep your arms out to balance yourself. Your shoulders, hips, knees and ankles should be relaxed and not in a stiff or locked position.

3. Put your weight on your forward foot and you should start to move.

4. As you turn, shift your weight in the direction you are going. You will either end up facing up the mountain or down the mountain.

5. If you are facing up the mountain, lean forward so your weight is on your toes. If you are facing down the mountain, lean back so your weight is on your heels.

6. If you want to stop while looking down the mountain, you can sit down. If you want to stop while looking up the mountain, you can kneel down. But make sure no one is close behind or you may cause a collision!

ARE YOU REGULAR OR GOOFY?

A regular boarder puts their left foot forward and their right foot at the back.

A goofy boarder puts their right foot forward and their left foot at the back.

You can test which one you are by climbing a set of stairs. Stand at the bottom. Whichever foot you naturally place on the first step should be the foot you put at the back of the board.

LEARN SOME LINGO FOR THE SLOPES

What is this boarder saying?

Dude, there's been a big dump and it'll be a bluebird tomorrow. Want to come and shred off-piste with the powder hounds?

Bluebird: a day of blue skies and fresh snow

Carving: a special skiing or snowboarding technique where the edges of the skis or snowboard cut into the snow

Dump: a big snowfall

Mogul: a small, hard mound of snow

Off-piste: an un-hardened and un-marked ski slope that is less safe for skiing

Piste: a hardened ski slope that is safe for skiing

Powder hound: someone who always hunts for untouched snow

Shred: if you shred the slope, you ski down it really well

White out: when the weather is bad, causing everyone to get stuck in a white cloud

Wipe out: falling over while skiing or snowboarding

SNOWSHOEING

Snowshoeing is like hiking, but
more difficult! You should only go
snowshoeing with a guide who
knows the mountain well and you must
wear the proper gear. That means special snowshoes
with metal spikes called 'crampons', and walking poles.

Going uphill, you need to take short steps and kick into
the snow to get a grip. If you find someone else's steps
from the day before, it's best not to use their path as it
might be icy.

Going downhill, you need
to 'plunge step'. Stand with
your feet shoulder-width
apart and bend your
knees. Then step down
the mountain
with your heel
slicing into the
snow first.

SURVIVAL TIP
Don't forget to
take plenty of water
and snacks on your
snow hike!

SURVIVING A SKI LIFT

There are different kinds of ski lift. The easiest to use is a 'bubble' or 'gondola', which takes you from one mountain to another. You need to take your skis or snowboard off, put them in the holder outside the bubble and get inside. You have to do this quite quickly while it is moving!

A 'chair lift' is a lift that you sit on. Before your chair lift is up in the air, make sure you and your fellow passengers have lowered the safety bar. Then enjoy the ride, and make sure you don't fall off.

A 'button' or 'drag' lift is usually quite a short lift. Instead of sitting down, you are dragged up the slope on your skis! When you reach the front of the queue, shuffle forward on your skis and wait for the button to swing around to you. When it reaches you, grab hold of the handle and place the button between your legs. The lift should pull you along. Make sure you don't sit down, or you'll fall over.

If you fall off the lift, don't worry! Get out of the way so you don't knock the person coming up behind you, then ski back down and have another go.

CROSS-COUNTRY SKIING

Cross-country skiing is a bit like a hike on skis! You must be very fit and strong and you'll also need special waxless skis that grip the snow with tiny scales, and a pair of long ski poles.

1. To start, practise by wearing just one ski. Push yourself along so you glide on the ski.

2. Once you've got used to gliding, put both skis on. Bend your knees and lean forward at the ankles. Your skis should be parallel, no more than hip-width apart.

REMEMBER
You will get very hot cross-country skiing, so always wear layers and take a rucksack in case you need to remove them.

3. Push off with your left foot and glide forward on your right ski. Then push off on your right ski and glide forward on your left ski. Keep repeating this push and glide movement.

4. Use your poles to push yourself along. Your arms should move in the opposite direction to your legs, so when you're gliding on your right leg, you should dig your left pole into the snow, and when you're gliding on your left leg, you should dig your right pole into the snow.

5. Try not to move the top half of your body too much or you will lose balance.

DID YOU KNOW?
An astronaut called Harrison Schmitt said that astronauts should learn how to cross country ski because he believed it would help them walk on the Moon more easily!

TOBOGGANING

REMEMBER
Try to avoid crashing into people, animals or trees!

Tobogganing is great fun! All you need is a toboggan and a helmet, which you should be able to rent from a ski shop. You will get sprayed with snow, so it's a good idea to wear warm, waterproof clothing and snowboots.

1. Carefully climb up the hill with your toboggan.

2. Sit on the toboggan with your feet up and your hands gripping the reins.

3. To steer, gently dig your heels into the snow.

4. To turn left, put your left heel into the snow. To turn right, put your right heel into the snow.

5. To slow down, dig both feet into the snow.

BUMBOARDING

Bumboarding is a bit like tobogganing, but even easier. All you need is a plastic bumboard or tray and a good slope. Avoid slopes with skiers or snowboarders, or you might have a nasty collision.

1. Walk up your slope.

2. Position yourself so you are sitting on your bumboard, holding the handle and with your legs on either side.

3. Launch yourself by raising your feet out of the snow. Now enjoy the ride!

4. To slow down and stop, dig your heels into the snow.

HOW NOT TO BUMBOARD:
standing up; with your dog on your lap; straight into your friend; straight into anyone!

BUILDING AN IGLOO

Igloos are shelters made from snow. They are great fun to make, but you will need a friend (or several) to help.

1. Find an area of hard-packed snow.

2. Cut out blocks of snow with a spade. The ideal snow block size is about 35 cm long, 8 cm wide and 20 cm deep. You can use a freezer tray as a mould.

3. Create an area of flat snow to build your igloo on, then draw a circle with your shoe or a spade.

4. Place the first layer of snow blocks around the circle.

5. Create a slope by scraping a diagonal section of snow from the top of each snow block.

6. Add more blocks to the bottom layer, following your slope around in a spiral. The more layers you add, the closer the walls should become. Make sure the blocks don't sit exactly in line with the edge of the blocks underneath them. Your igloo will be stronger if the blocks on top slightly overlap the blocks below.

7. As you build, trim the insides of the blocks so they slant inward.

8. The final block should be placed in the hole at the top — it will hold in place if it's wider at the top.

9. Dig an entrance into the snow wall on the side facing away from the wind.

MOUNTAIN FACTS

1. The highest peak on Earth is Mount Everest, but the tallest mountain is Mauna Kea in Hawaii. It's not as high as Everest because it starts deep under the sea!

2. You can find fossils of sea animals and seashells high up in some mountains. These fossils formed under the sea millions of years ago, and were then carried to the peaks as the mountains formed.

3. There are many mountains in the world that haven't yet been climbed.

4. In 1924, George Mallory and Sandy Irvine died trying to climb Everest. Experts are not certain whether they were on their way up or down when they died. The mystery could one day be solved if someone finds Irvine's body and the camera he was carrying.

5. Other planets have mountains too. The tallest that we know of is on Mars. It is called Olympus Mons and it's 24 kilometres tall.

6. Himalayan jumping spiders are the highest-living creatures we know of, living 22,000 feet up Mount Everest.

7. There are four enormous heads carved into Mount Rushmore in the USA. They are of four American presidents and were carved in the 1920s and 30s.

8. Some people have adapted to live in the mountains. The Quechua Indians in the Andes have extra blood vessels in their feet, enabling them to walk barefoot in the freezing cold.

9. Mount Everest grows about 4 mm every year because the plates of the Earth's crust are pushing against each other.

10. Henriette D'Angeville, who climbed Mont Blanc in the Alps in 1838, had to wear a long skirt during her trek! She wore a pair of warm trousers underneath though.

TOP TIP
If you find a fossil, you can draw it, trace its shape or make a rubbing!

WHAT TO SEE IN THE MOUNTAINS

BIRDS

GOLDEN EAGLES
are large
dark-brown
birds of prey, with a
golden head and neck
and patterned underwings.
They are very large, with a
wingspan as wide as a tall grown-up.

KESTRELS have large, pointed
wings and a long black-tipped
tail. Males have a spotted,
reddish-brown back, while
females are brown with black
markings. All kestrels make a
shrill, rasping noise.

PEREGRINE FALCONS are powerful
birds of prey. They are mostly
blue-grey, with a black head
and a white throat and cheeks.
They wait for prey while perched
high up, then dive quickly and
steeply, using their talons to kill.

PTARMIGANS are small
birds that make a dry,
croaking noise. In the
summer they are greyish-
brown and black with a
white belly and wings.
In the winter, they turn
completely white except
for their black tail and
eye patch.

ALPINE CHOUGHS are
small, black birds
with a yellow bill and
red legs. They fly
in flocks and make
strange sizzling or
hissing noises.

BAR-HEADED GEESE live in
Asia and they cross the
Himalayas when they
migrate. That makes
them the highest-flying
bird species in
the world.

MAMMALS

It's hard for most animals to survive in the mountains because it's cold and windy, and food is difficult to find. So mountain animals have adapted to suit the extreme conditions.

CHAMOIS are a type of mountain goat. In summer, they have brown fur and in winter it turns light grey. They have white patches on their head and short horns. They like to slide down snowy slopes on their bottom, steering with their legs!

IBEX are also a type of mountain goat. They are slightly larger than chamois and have brownish-grey fur. Males have curved horns that can grow to over three feet. Female horns are shorter. They eat grass, leaves and flowers.

LYNX are wildcats
with brown,
beige or gold
fur, sometimes
patterned with
dark brown spots.
They have black
tufts of hair on the
tips of their ears
and their paws are

large and padded so they can walk on snow. Lynx eat
lots of different animals, from mountain goats and deer
to birds and fish.

MOUNTAIN LIONS
are bigger than
cats but smaller
than lions. They
can jump up to
five metres high
(that's about
the size of three
grown-ups) and

are very dangerous. They are not found in Europe, but
if you're ever hiking in North, Central or South America,
you should know how to act if you come across one.
The worst things you can do are run away, crouch down
or turn your back on it. Instead, make yourself look very
big by raising your jumper or jacket over your head and
shouting in a deep, loud voice.

BEARS are amazing animals, but very dangerous. Bears were last seen in the UK about 1,300 years ago, but if you're hiking in a

country where there are bears, do NOT leave food lying around. If you see a bear, stay calm. Don't run, make sudden movements or climb a tree. Slowly step away with your eyes on the bear and speak in a low voice. If it looks like it might attack, shout, flap your arms and make yourself look big.

GREY WOLVES are very shy and usually avoid humans, but if one approaches you, don't run, look it in the eye or show your teeth. Instead, you should make yourself look very big and try to climb a tree or a rock. If the wolf attacks, fight back and aim for its nose.

MOUNTAIN HARES are larger than rabbits, but smaller than normal hares. In the summer their fur is greyish-brown. In winter it turns completely white, except for their black ear tips. They eat grass, twigs and bark.

MARMOTS are giant squirrels that live in the mountains and hibernate in burrows for most of the winter. They have brown or reddish-brown fur, short legs and strong claws for digging. If they are scared they let out a piercing whistle.

PINE MARTENS have slim bodies, bushy tails and thick, dark brown fur with yellow throat patches. They are very good at climbing and eat small animals, insects and fruit.

TRACKING MOUNTAIN ANIMALS

1. What can you smell?
2. Can you find any tracks?
3. Can you find any animal wee or poo? (If you do, DON'T TOUCH IT!)

REMEMBER:

• Be as quiet as you can so you don't scare the animals.
• Stand downwind of the animals, so they can't smell you.
• Step from heel to toe as it helps to soften your step.
• The best times to track animals are early morning, late afternoon or early evening. This is when animals are most active!

HOW NOT TO TRACK ANIMALS:

doing the hokey cokey; singing a song; pretending to be a wild animal (they won't fall for it!)

IDENTIFYING MOUNTAIN ANIMAL TRACKS

CHAMOIS

IBEX

MOUNTAIN HARE

MARMOT

67

IDENTIFYING MOUNTAIN ANIMAL POO

Can you match the animals to the correct poo?

CHAMOIS

BEAR

GREY WOLF

PINE MARTEN

1 Dark and coiled

2 Oblong-shaped pellets

3 Tube-shaped

4 Long with a tapered end and hair

PLANTS AND TREES

Mountain plants and trees have had to adapt to harsh environments. Many grow close to the ground to keep out of the wind, or have special ways to store food over the winter.

ALPINE ROCK JASMINE is a pink or white flower with green leaves that grows on rocky ground. It is hardy and can grow above 4,000 metres in very cold temperatures.

GLACIER BUTTERCUPS are found on the banks of mountain rivers. Their flowers look similar to a normal buttercup, but with paler yellow petals.

RUSTY-LEAVED ALPENROSES have clusters of bright pink, bell-shaped flowers with rusty-coloured spots on their undersides.

ALPINE SNOWBELLS have purple bell-shaped flowers, which poke out of the snow in early spring. They look harmless but if you touch one it will burn your fingers.

EDELWEISS is a white flower covered in hair, which protects it from the cold. In some countries it is given as a promise of dedication to loved ones.

FOXGLOVES grow on rocky mountain slopes. Their flowers are purple-pink or white with spots and are very poisonous.

MOUNTAIN SORREL has tall clusters of green flowers that turn red when they ripen. Its tufts of heart-shaped leaves are full of Vitamin C and are sometimes added to salads.

PYRENEAN LILY is a plant with beautiful yellow cup-shaped flowers and spiky green leaves. It grows up to 1.3 metres tall and has a very bad smell.

SWISS PINES are
tall trees with
drooping
branches
and thin trunks.
They grow slowly but
can live up to 1,000
years. They have
needle-like leaves and
historically their sap
was sometimes used
to make drinks in
the spring.

MACEDONIAN PINES are tall
trees with needle-like
leaves. They can survive
very cold temperatures
and produce a liquid
called resin, which
was used in the past
to treat wounds.

WHAT TO DO IF YOU GET INTO TROUBLE IN THE MOUNTAINS

Anything can happen when you're going wild in the mountains. You or someone in your team might feel unwell or fall and break a bone. Here's how to help.

MOUNTAIN RESCUE

Before you go into the mountains, make sure you have the contact details for the closest mountain rescue team. Their job is to help people in emergencies, whether someone has broken a bone or fallen down an icy crevasse. They travel via helicopter, snowmobile or on skis.

ALTITUDE SICKNESS

DID YOU KNOW?
If you climb Mount Everest, you may have to take oxygen to help you breathe.

If you climb a high mountain you may reach altitudes where there is less oxygen in the air. Lack of oxygen can make you feel tired, dizzy and sick. You might even start seeing or hearing things that are not really there. To avoid altitude sickness, mountaineers climb up mountains gradually, so their bodies get used to the reduction in oxygen.

Luckily, you will probably not be venturing into the 'death zone' on your trip to the mountains. This is the height where there is not enough oxygen to keep you alive, usually above 8,000 metres.

HYPOTHERMIA

If it's very, very cold, you must make sure you're wearing enough clothes. If you don't, you might get hypothermia. This is when your body temperature drops below normal. You will start shivering and become clumsy, confused and sleepy. Your speech will slur, and your fingers, toes, lips and ears will turn blue.

If you think you have hypothermia, you must warm up gradually. Try to light a fire and huddle like penguins with your teammates. You should also try to get medical help as soon as possible. Contact mountain rescue or alert anyone nearby to help.

To avoid getting hypothermia, follow these top tips:

1. Keep your head, neck and hands covered and warm.

2. Keep your clothes as dry as possible.

3. Make sure you eat enough food and snacks.

4. Keep active.

5. Drink lots of water.

FROSTBITE

Another reason to make sure you're wrapped up warm is to avoid getting frostbite! If your body becomes extremely cold, parts of your skin will start to freeze. This usually happens on your fingers, toes, ears and nose.

First, your skin will turn red and feel very cold to touch. After a while, it will go numb or prickly, then it will turn a paler colour and might go blue. You might see ice crystals forming on your skin. If you don't warm up it will turn blue and blood-filled blisters will develop. The area might feel like a block of wood.

If you're worried you might be getting frostbite, you should start warming up that area. Swing your arms around like windmill sails and wiggle your toes. Tuck your hands under your armpits to keep them warm and huddle with your friends. Get medical help as soon as possible.

HOW TO BANDAGE A WOUND

1. Control the bleeding by pressing or wrapping a clean cloth over the wound.

2. Gently remove anything that is stuck in the wound.

3. Clean the wound with plain soap and clean water. You could also use a disinfectant wipe.

4. Press a sanitised (straight from the wrapper) bandage to the wound.

5. If you don't have any bandages, you can use a piece of clean cloth.

6. Secure the dressing with water-resistant, non-stretch medical tape and cover it.

7. Change the dressing daily.

DID YOU KNOW?
Saliva (spit) can be used to help clean a wound in an emergency. But don't spit on anyone without their permission!

BROKEN BONES AND SPRAINS

If someone breaks a bone or sprains their ankle or wrist, they will be in a lot of pain. Do not annoy them or try to give them a relaxing massage. The best thing to do is to try to reduce the swelling. If you have something cold like a wet cloth or some snow, place this on the break or sprain. Next, find a crutch for them to lean on. Then call for help! Mountain rescue might take them down the mountain in a 'blood wagon', which is a stretcher carried by the rescue team on skis.

WHAT TO DO IF YOU GET CAUGHT IN AN AVALANCHE

An avalanche is a large mass of snow that suddenly comes loose and tumbles down the mountain. If you're up in the mountains when it's snowy, you must know what to do if you're hit by one.

The best way to avoid an avalanche is to only ski or snowboard on pisted runs, and to always check the conditions before you set out.

If an avalanche is coming from behind you, don't try to escape it by racing down the mountain. It will move faster than you! Instead, aim for the side of the mountain slope. This way, you may be able to get out of its path before it reaches you. Remove any heavy equipment so you are as light and fast as possible.

If you're unable to escape an avalanche, see if you can shelter behind a tree or a boulder. Cover your mouth so you don't swallow any snow.

The best way to stop yourself being buried in the snow is to start swimming in it, as if you're swimming uphill. This might sound silly, but it will help you stay near the surface of the snow rather than sinking underneath it.

You might not be sure which way is up after an avalanche. A good way to find out is to spit. If you feel the spit dribbling down your chin, you're the right way up. If it dribbles across your face, you are upside down.

If you can move, try to dig yourself out of the snow. If you have a ski pole, try to stick it up toward the surface of the slope. Any clothing or equipment visible on the surface will help the rescue team to find you.

DID YOU KNOW?
Most ski resorts use special cannons to safely set off avalanches when no one is on the mountain. This releases build-ups of snow, so dangerous avalanches are less likely to occur.

Rescue dogs are also excellent at finding people after avalanches.

HOW TO AVOID FALLING DOWN A CREVASSE

A crevasse is a deep crack in the ice. They can be found on glaciers, which are big areas of thick ice that slowly move. Crevasses are incredibly deep and dangerous and are often hidden by snow.

To avoid falling down a crevasse, go nowhere near one. They are usually roped off, but there might be undiscovered crevasses, so it's good to know how to identify them.

In the summer, this is much easier because they are visible. However, when it's snowy, crevasses might be hidden. You might be able to spot shadows or shapes in the snow, but often the only way to check for crevasses is to prod the snow ahead of you with a pole.

If anyone in your group falls down a crevasse, call mountain rescue straight away!

GETTING LOST IN THE MOUNTAINS

If you're stuck outside in the cold, you absolutely must keep calm and stay warm.

If possible, make sure your fingers, toes, ears and nose are covered, and try to keep moving your arms and legs or huddle with your teammates, around a fire if possible.

Speak to the rest of the team and check that they are OK. See if there is anyone nearby who might be able to help you. If no one is about, call mountain rescue. Whatever you do, don't split up from your team!

MOUNTAIN QUIZ

1. Which mountain mammal likes to slide down snowy slopes on its bottom?
> A) Lynx
> B) Chamois
> C) Hare

2. What is the highest mountain on Earth?
> A) The Matterhorn
> B) Mount Kilimanjaro
> C) Mount Everest

3. What are the shoes with metal spikes on them for snowshoeing called?
> A) Crampons
> B) Plunge shoes
> C) Spikees

4. When you go rock climbing, where should you put your body weight?
> A) Your arms
> B) Your legs
> C) Your hands

5. Which mountain flower is covered in hairs to protect it from the cold?
> A) Edelweiss
> B) Foxglove
> C) Alpine snowbell

6. What is the name for a ski slope that has been hardened so it is safe for skiing?
    A) Mogul
    B) Bluebird
    C) Piste

7. What bird flies over the Himalayas and is the highest-flying bird in the world?
    A) Bar-headed goose
    B) Peregrine falcon
    C) Alpine chough

8. What should you do if you're approached by a grey wolf?
    A) Look it straight in the eye and crouch down low
    B) Make yourself look big and climb up a tree
    C) Stand on one leg and make bird noises

9. What is the name for the ape-like creature with a shaggy white coat that people claim to have seen in the Himalayas?
    A) Snark
    B) Himalayabeast
    C) Yeti

10. What shape should your skis make when you ski snow plough?
    A) An orange shape
    B) A pizza shape
    C) A railway line shape

MAGNIFICENT MOUNTAINS

We hope you have a marvellous time in the mountains. They can be magical places, whether you're admiring the view from a snowy mountain peak or watching a family of chamois hopping across the grass.

While it's great fun to go wild in the mountains, it's most important to be respectful of this beautiful space. That means following the rules, listening to your grown-ups and being careful not to disturb the environment. As the saying goes, you should leave only footprints and take only memories!

GLOSSARY

Altitude A measurement of distance or height above a chosen point, usually sea level.

Altitude sickness An illness that mountain climbers can get upon reaching altitudes where there is less oxygen in the air.

Bearing The direction in which your destination lies.

Blizzard An intense and dangerous snowstorm with strong winds.

Compass A tool that uses magnetised needles to show the direction of magnetic north. It helps users to work out the direction in which they need to go.

Dehydrate To feel weak or ill because you don't have enough water in your body. It can be very dangerous to be dehydrated.

Downstream A word to describe the direction in which a river or stream is flowing.

Dry ski slope A ski slope made of materials that act like snow but that can be skied on even when the weather isn't cold.

Global Positioning System (GPS) A worldwide system that uses satellites to allow people to work out exactly where they are, how fast they are going and what time it is.

Hardy Able to survive difficult weather or environmental conditions (e.g. the snow or high altitudes).

Harness A type of equipment used in rock climbing that protects a climber by connecting them to a stable point or rope.

Life jacket A sleeveless vest that can keep a person afloat in water.

Mammals Warm-blooded animals with hair and a spine or backbone. Humans are mammals.

Navigation The process of working out your position and how to get from that position to your destination.

Parallel Being the same width apart and never connecting.

Penknife A small knife that can fold up and be easily carried.

Reel A piece of fishing equipment that attaches to the handle of a fishing rod to allow a fishing line to be cast out to the water and reeled in towards the fisher.

Stagnant water Water that is not moving or flowing.

Tarp or tarpaulin A heavy, waterproof cloth that can be used as protection from wet, windy weather.

Toboggan A type of sled that can be used to slide downhill on snow or ice.

Water purification tablets Tablets that can be added to water to make it safer for humans to drink.

INDEX